SIMPLY

Tennessee

by

Betty Jane McClanahan

McClanahan
Publishing House

All order correspondence should be addressed to:

McClanahan Publishing House, Inc.
P.O. Box 100
Kuttawa, KY 42055
(502) 388-9388
800-544-6959

Other books by McClanahan Publishing House, Inc.

A Little Touch of Grace
American Sampler Cookbook
Assassination at the State House
Castle: The Story of a Kentucky Prison
Cook Talk with Curtis Grace & Friends
Cooking with Curtis Grace
Crazy About the Cats
Cunningham Family History Book
Dining in Historic Georgia
Dining in Historic Kentucky
Dining in Historic Ohio
Dining in the Historic South
Especially Herbs
Flames in the Wind
Kentucky's Clark
Ky. College Basketball NAMES & GAMES
Lake Superior's North Shore in Good Taste
Lexington in Good Taste
Louisville in Good Taste
Nuts About Pecans
On Bended Knees: The Night Rider Story
Sample West Kentucky
Savor Superior
Whitehaven: The Rebirth of a Southern Mansion

Dedication

This book is dedicated to Paula Cunningham, a wonderful friend who happens to be a cousin. What fun we've had traveling together and sampling great foods prepared by interesting friends. Her encouragement to write this book is appreciated.

Table of Contents

*R*emember,
anything tastes
better served in a
pretty dish!

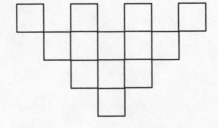

Quesadillas

½ cup melted margarine
8 8-inch flour tortillas
1½ cups grated Monterey Jack cheese
1½ cups grated cheddar cheese
8 ounces salsa

Pour 2 tablespoons melted margarine in plate and coat tortilla on one side, spread with ¾ cup mixed cheeses. Top with 2 tablespoons salsa, dip second tortilla in melted margarine and place over the tortilla with the mixture on it. Repeat process until 4 quesadillas are made. Heat skillet over low heat. Carefully slip one prepared quesadilla into skillet. Cook on one side 2 to 3 minutes, then carefully turn to brown on the other side. Remove from skillet and cut into 4 to 6 pieces. Serve with guacamole, sour cream and salsa. Serves 6 to 8.

Shrimp Mold

1½ envelopes unflavored gelatin
8 ounces cream cheese
¾ cup chopped celery
1 cup mayonnaise
1 small onion, finely chopped
Lemon juice, to taste
2 cups cooked shrimp
Salt
Pepper

Soften gelatin in ½ cup cold water. Whip cream cheese and add softened gelatin. Dissolve over low heat. Fold in remaining ingredients. Place in mold (fish mold is best). Chill until firm. Serve with crackers.

Layered Taco Dip

16 ounces refried beans
4¼ ounces chopped ripe olives, drained
4 ounces chopped green chilies
6 ounces avocado dip
8 to 10 green onions, chopped
2 tomatoes, chopped
1 cup shredded cheddar cheese
1 carton sour cream

Layer all ingredients in a bowl in the order listed. Serve with chips of your choice. Makes 8 cups.

Cheese Fondue

1 pound Swiss cheese
1 cup sauterne wine
Garlic salt
French bread

Coat Swiss cheese in a little flour. Heat wine in fondue pot, add cheese and garlic salt. Stir until smooth. Break bread into bite-size pieces; dip bread into cheese mixture.

*A*dd some chunky peanut butter, banana and raisins to cooked, hot oatmeal for a special cold morning treat for breakfast. Kids will notice.

Spinach Dip

10 ounces frozen chopped spinach, thawed
8 ounces sour cream
½ cup mayonnaise
8 ounces water chestnuts, drained and chopped
1 package Knorr's vegetable soup mix

Drain spinach. Combine all ingredients, cover and refrigerate.

Country Ham Balls

1 pound ground cooked country ham
½ pound sausage
½ cup dry bread crumbs
1 egg
Small amount of milk
2 cups brown sugar
1 tablespoon prepared mustard
1 cup water
1 cup white vinegar

Mix ham, sausage, crumbs and egg together. Add enough milk to roll into small balls. Place in a 9 x 13 inch pan, sprayed with Pam. In a saucepan, add sugar, mustard, water and vinegar. Bring to a boil. Pour ½ of the sauce over balls and bake at 400° for 45 minutes, or until firm. Use remaining sauce to pour over ham balls for serving.

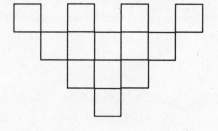

Easy Boiled Custard

3¾ ounces French Vanilla instant pudding mix
4 cups milk
½ cup sugar
1 teaspoon vanilla
8 ounces Cool Whip

Combine pudding mix, milk, sugar and vanilla. Stir until smooth. Fold in whipped topping. Chill until very, very cold.

* This recipe comes from my good friend, Curtis Grace, caterer and restaurant owner from Paducah, Kentucky.

Orange Julius

6 ounces frozen orange juice
1 teaspoon vanilla
½ cup sugar
1 cup water
1 cup milk
10 to 12 ice cubes

Combine all ingredients in blender.

Add a splash of vanilla
extract along with your
freshly ground coffee
beans before brewing that
morning coffee. Also,
invest in a plug-in timer—
what a luxury to smell
fresh coffee perking before
you get out of bed!

Great Instant Cocoa Mix

1 8 quart box instant milk
1 box confectioners' sugar
8 tablespoons cocoa
1 6 ounce jar instant coffee creamer
1 pound box Nestle's chocolate drink mix

Mix all of the above ingredients. To serve, add ⅓ cup to 1 cup of hot water.

Hot Mulled Cider

2 quarts apple cider
¼ cup brown sugar
2 sticks cinnamon
1 teaspoon cloves
1 orange, sliced

Combine the above ingredients in a crock pot or slow cooker.
Let cook for 2 to 5 hours. Serves 10 to 12.

*I*f your brown sugar
becomes hard when
stored, place a slice of
bread in the container
and it will become
soft again.

Sangria
(Wine Punch)

1 cup sugar
2 cups water
1 orange, thinly sliced
2 limes, thinly sliced
1 bottle red wine

Boil sugar and water 5 minutes; while hot, add orange slices and lime slices. Let stand at least 4 hours.

To serve: place ice cubes in a glass pitcher. Add 6 thinly sliced oranges, 6 thinly sliced limes and ½ cup of the above syrup. Add wine to fill pitcher.

Banana Punch

6 bananas, mashed
48 ounces unsweetened pineapple juice
2 cups sugar
6 cups water
24 ounces frozen orange juice
12 ounces frozen lemonade
3 liter bottle Sprite or 7-up

Mix bananas and pineapple juice. Add sugar, water, orange juice and lemonade. Pour into containers and freeze.

When ready to serve: remove mixture from containers and pour Sprite or 7-up over frozen mixture; stir until slushy.

Tennessee Tea

One 2-gallon tea bag
or 3 heaping tablespoons loose tea leaves
24 ounces frozen orange juice
Juice of 8 lemons
2 pounds sugar
Pinch of dry mint leaves

Steep tea in a small amount of boiling water. Remove from heat.

In a separate container, combine orange juice, lemon juice, sugar and mint leaves. Combine tea and juices; add enough cold water to make 2 gallons. Strain before serving.

Breads

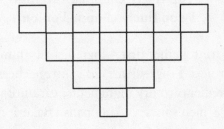

Zucchini Cornbread

3 cups corn meal
½ cup plain flour
2 teaspoons baking powder
½ teaspoon salt
1½ cups cottage cheese
1½ cups milk
1 cup melted butter
4 eggs
1 cup finely chopped zucchini
1 cup finely chopped onion

In large bowl, stir together first 4 ingredients. In medium bowl, whisk together next 4 ingredients, add cottage cheese and remaining ingredients to dry ingredients; stir until moist. Pour into 2 greased 8-inch square baking pans. Bake at 375° for 23 to 30 minutes.

Hush Puppies

1 cup self-rising flour
1 cup cornmeal
1 onion, finely chopped
1 cup buttermilk
1 egg
¼ teaspoon sugar
¼ teaspoon salt

Mix all ingredients, drop in deep fat, cook until brown.

*I*f you're planning to serve seafood to guests, check to make sure no one is allergic to it.

I learned the hard way!

Spoon Rolls

1 package dry yeast
2 cups lukewarm water
4 cups self-rising flour
¾ cup melted shortening
¼ cup sugar
1 egg

Dissolve yeast in water. Mix together in a large bowl with other
ingredients. Store, covered, in refrigerator and use as desired.
This batter keeps several days.*

To use: spoon batter into well-greased muffin tins. Bake at 425°
for 20 minutes.

*You do not have to wait for these to rise.

Flower Pot Bread

6 3-inch clay flower pots
1 package active dry yeast
½ cup warm water
3 tablespoons sugar, divided
13 ounces evaporated milk
1 teaspoon salt
2 tablespoons vegetable oil
4 to 4½ cups plain flour

Season pots by baking at 425° for 30 minutes, grease well with vegetable oil and repeat.

Dissolve yeast in water, add 1 tablespoon sugar. Let stand 15 minutes, add remaining sugar, milk, salt and oil. Beat in flour, 1 cup at a time. Fill pots ½ full. Let dough rise. Bake at 350° for 40 to 45 minutes. When done, brush tops with butter and let cool 5 to 10 minutes. Loosen crust with a knife.

Orange Blossom Muffins

12 ounces frozen orange juice concentrate, thawed
½ cup sugar
4 tablespoons oil
2 eggs beaten
4 cups Bisquick
1 cup orange marmalade
1 cup granola or chopped, toasted pecans

Combine juice, sugar, oil and eggs. Add Bisquick, marmalade and nuts and pour into 12 greased muffin tins. Bake at 400° for 20 minutes.

Best Ever No-Fat Muffins

1½ cups self rising flour
¾ cup brown sugar
½ cup grated apple, peeled or try canned drained peaches,
mashed banana, drained fruit cocktail, etc.
2 teaspoons cinnamon
⅔ cup skim milk
⅔ cup plain, low fat yogurt

Combine flour, sugar, apple, cinnamon and mix well. Gently stir
in milk and yogurt, just until mixed, then pour into 12 greased
muffin tins and bake at 400° for 15 minutes or until brown.
Try ¼ cup preserves for an added treat!

Yogurt Raisin Bran Muffins

2 cups Raisin Bran cereal
1 cup skim milk
½ cup plain yogurt
1¼ cups self-rising flour
½ cup brown sugar
½ teaspoon soda
1 teaspoon cinnamon

Mix cereal and milk and let stand. Meanwhile mix together flour, sugar, soda, and cinnamon. Add dry mixture to cereal, milk, then yogurt and gently stir until mixed. Pour into 12 greased muffin tins and bake at 400° for 20 minutes or until brown.

Variation: Add ¼ cup strawberry preserves and 2 teaspoons cinnamon. Bake as usual.

Eggs

Quiche

Pastry for 9-inch pie
8 slices bacon
½ cup green onions
6 eggs, beaten
1 cup grated Swiss cheese
2 cups Half & Half

Mix all the above ingredients. Pour into pastry. Bake at 375° for 35 to 45 minutes. Serves 6.

Sausage and Egg Casserole

6 slices white bread
½ pound sliced American cheese
1 pound sausage, cooked and drained
4 eggs, beaten
2 cups milk
½ teaspoon dry mustard
Dash Worcestershire sauce

Line a greased casserole dish with bread. Spread cheese over bread. Beat eggs, adding milk, mustard, and Worcestershire sauce. Add sausage; pour egg mixture over all ingredients. Let set 1 to 2 hours. Bake, covered, at 350° for 1 hour; uncovering during the last 10 minutes of baking time.

Egg Casserole

3 tablespoons butter
3 tablespoons flour
1 cup milk
1 teaspoon salt
1 teaspoon Worcestershire sauce
¼ onion, grated
8 hard-boiled eggs, grated
Chicken chunks
¼ pound cheese, grated

Combine butter and flour in a saute pan; add milk, salt,
Worcestershire sauce and onion; cook until thick. In a 1-quart
baking dish, layer sauce, eggs and chicken; top with cheese.
Bake at 325° for 25 minutes.

Ham and Eggs Pizza

8 ounces refrigerator crescent rolls
¼ cup chopped onions
1 tablespoon melted butter
1 cup chopped ham
1 cup shredded Swiss cheese
4 large eggs, lightly beaten
½ cup milk
Salt and pepper

Unroll rolls and place in a 9 x 13 pan. Press ½ inch up sides of pan to form a crust. Press together all perforations. Bake at 375° for 5 minutes. Set aside.

Saute onions in butter over medium heat; add ham. Spread over dough and sprinkle with cheese. Mix together eggs, milk, salt and pepper; pour over cheese. Bake at 350° for 25 to 30 minutes.

Soups, Salads, Salad Dressings & Sauces

Bread Bowls for Salads

16 ounces hot roll mix
1 cup instant mashed potato flakes
2 tablespoons dried minced onion
1⅓ cups hot water
2 tablespoons melted butter
1 egg
Vegetable cooking spray

Combine all ingredients in large mixing bowl. Knead in bowl
until you can form a soft ball, turn onto lightly floured surface
and knead about 5 minutes. Cover and let rest 5 minutes.

On large baking sheet, invert 6 ovenproof custard cups. Spray
with cooking spray, divide dough into 6 portions. Shape dough
over each cup and spray with cooking spray. Cover and let rise in
a warm place about 45 minutes. Bake at 375° for 25 minutes or
until golden brown. While warm, remove from cups; let cool and
store in an airtight container. Serves 6.

Shrimp Bisque

1 pound medium-size fresh shrimp
3 tablespoons butter or margarine
3 tablespoons all-purpose flour
1 medium onion, chopped
2 stalks celery
2 cloves garlic, crushed
1 sweet red pepper, coarsely chopped
4 cups fish stock
8 ounces tomato sauce
2 to 3 dashes hot sauce
1 bay leaf
¼ teaspoon paprika
Fresh chives, for garnish

Peel and devein shrimp; set aside. Melt butter in a Dutch oven over medium heat; add flour, stirring until smooth. Cook, stirring constantly, 5 minutes, or until mixture is golden brown. Stir in onion, celery and garlic; cook, stirring constantly, 3 minutes. Add red pepper and cook 1 minute. Gradually add stock and next 4 ingredients. Bring to a boil, stirring constantly. Reduce heat and simmer 5 minutes. Add shrimp and cook 5 minutes or until shrimp turn pink. Remove and discard bay leaf. Spoon into individual bowls; garnish, if desired. Yields 6½ cups.

Clam Chowder

1 small onion, chopped
1 stick margarine
2 to 4 cans minced clams, drained
5 cans cream of potato soup
3 cans English clam chowder
½ gallon Half & Half

Saute onions in butter. Combine all ingredients and bake in a heavy covered Dutch oven at 200° for 4 hours, stirring occasionally. Makes 7 quarts.

Note: This recipe freezes well.

New England Corn Chowder

½ pound bacon
2 onions, chopped
2 tablespoons plain flour
4 cups water
6 to 8 medium potatoes, cubed
17 ounces cream-style corn
12 ounces evaporated milk
Salt and pepper
2 tablespoons butter

Cook bacon in large Dutch oven until crisp, remove bacon and saute onions in bacon fat, add flour and stir. Add water and potatoes, bring to boil. Cover and simmer until potatoes are tender. Add corn, milk, and season to taste with salt and pepper. Add butter; heat thoroughly but do not boil. Stir in bacon. Makes 2 quarts.

Apricot Salad

6 ounces orange Jello
2 cups boiling water
20 ounces cut apricots
20 ounces pineapple tidbits
10 marshmallows

Topping:
1 cup pineapple/apricot juice
½ cup sugar
2½ tablespoons flour
1 egg, beaten
2 tablespoons butter
Grated cheese, optional

Mix Jello and water until Jello is dissolved. Drain apricots and pineapples, reserving juices from both. Combine juices and measure 1 cup; set aside remainder. Add apricots, pineapple and juice to Jello and stir. Add marshmallows.

Cook topping ingredients until thickened. Spread over gelatin mixture. Top with grated cheese, if desired.

Cranberry Jello Salad

2 cups cranberries
1¼ cups cold water
1 cup sugar
3 ounces cherry Jello
½ cup chopped celery
1 apple, chopped
½ cup chopped nuts

Cook cranberries in 1 cup water for 20 minutes, add sugar. Soften Jello in remaining ¼ cup water. Combine cranberries, Jello and remaining ingredients; turn into mold and chill.

Mexican Chef Salad

1 pound ground beef
15 ounces kidney beans, drained
¼ teaspoon salt
1 onion, chopped
4 tomatoes, chopped
1 head of lettuce, torn
4 ounces shredded cheddar cheese
Tortilla chips, crushed
1 large avocado, sliced
Thousand Island dressing, to taste
Hot sauce, to taste

Brown ground beef and onion; add kidney beans and salt.
Simmer for 10 minutes. Combine tomatoes and lettuce.
Toss with cheddar cheese, dressing and hot sauce. Add tortilla
chips, sliced avocado and add hot meat mixture at the last
minute. Serves 6 to 8.

A quick salad dressing is made by combining picante sauce, or salsa, with mayonnaise. Experiment, the flavors are spicy and nice.

Scandinavian Salad

16 ounces English peas, drained
16 ounces French cut green beans, drained
1 small jar chopped pimiento
4 large stalks celery, chopped
1 medium purple onion, chopped
½ cup salad oil
1 cup red vinegar
1 tablespoon salt
1 cup sugar
1 teaspoon paprika

Mix all vegetables in large bowl. Combine salad oil, vinegar, salt, sugar and paprika; pour over vegetables. Let stand in refrigerator 24 hours. Drain and serve.

Zesty Dressing

½ cup salad oil
3 tablespoons vinegar
½ small onion, chopped
2 tablespoons minced parsley
1 tablespoon minced green pepper
1 teaspoon powdered sugar
1 teaspoon salt
1 teaspoon dry mustard
½ teaspoon red pepper

Mix all ingredients in a blender. Serve over green salad.

If someone does not care for certain vegetables in their salad, slice vegetables in larger sections so that they can easily pick them out (onions, celery, cucumbers, etc.)

Tennessee Barbecue Sauce
for Chicken

2 cups cider vinegar
4 tablespoons salt
½ bottle Tabasco sauce
3 tablespoons Worcestershire sauce
¼ teaspoon garlic powder

Combine all ingredients in saucepan and bring to a rolling boil. (This is better if made the day before using.) Brush chicken liberally with sauce while grilling.

Tomato Aspic

2½ envelopes unflavored gelatin
1 quart tomato juice
1 quart Snap-E-Tom juice
3 stalks chopped celery
½ onion
Juice of 1 lemon
½ teaspoon salt
3 to 5 drops Tabasco sauce

Optional ingredients:
Sliced olives
Cottage cheese
Green onions, chopped
Green pepper, chopped
Red peppers, chopped
Celery, chopped

Soften gelatin in ½ pint cold tomato juice. Simmer remainder of ingredients 30 minutes. Strain; add gelatin and your preference of optional ingredients. Pour into mold, depending on what you added, chill and serve.

Spinach Salad

¾ cup wine vinegar
1 tablespoon soy sauce
¼ cup sugar
¾ cup chili sauce
Fresh spinach
Bacon bits
Grated hard-boiled eggs

Combine all liquid ingredients for dressing. Wash spinach. Toss with dressing. Top with bacon bits and grated eggs. Sliced onion rings may be added.

Spinach Salad

1½ pounds fresh spinach
3 boiled eggs, chopped
8 ounces water chestnuts, sliced and drained
6 slices bacon, fried and crumbled
½ red onion, sliced thinly

Dressing:
½ cup vegetable oil
⅓ cup sugar
⅓ cup catsup
¼ cup vinegar
2 tablespoons sherry
1 teaspoon salt
1 teaspoon paprika
1 teaspoon A-1 sauce
1 tablespoon minced onion

Combine all salad ingredients. Combine all dressing ingredients
in blender and toss with salad.

Cucumber Mold

2 cucumbers
1 envelope unflavored gelatin
½ cup cold water
3 ounces lime Jello
1¼ cups boiling water
½ cup lemon juice
1 tablespoon grated onion
½ teaspoon salt
⅛ teaspoon cayenne pepper
½ cup chopped celery
¼ cup chopped parsley
½ pint whipping cream, whipped

Peel and coarsely grate cucumbers. Soften gelatin in cold water and dissolve lime Jello in boiling water. Add gelatin mixture to lime Jello. Stir in lemon juice, onion, salt and cayenne pepper. Chill to partially thickened. Fold cucumber, celery, parsley and whipped cream into thickened gelatin. Pour into a 4-cup mold, chill until firm. Serves 4 to 6.

Curried Broccoli Salad

2 bunches broccoli
2 to 2½ cups red grapes
½ red onion, diced
½ cup slivered almonds, toasted
1 cup mayonnaise
9 ounces chutney
2 teaspoons curry powder

Cut broccoli into florets. Discard bottom half of stem. Peel and dice remaining upper portion. Place broccoli, along with washed and plucked red grapes, red onion and almonds in large bowl. In separate bowl, combine mayonnaise, chutney and curry powder; mix thoroughly. Add to broccoli mixture and blend well. Refrigerate 1 hour before serving to let flavors blend. Serve in your favorite glass bowl. Makes 6 to 8 servings.

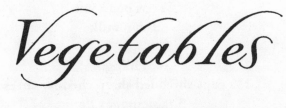

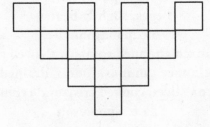

Florentine Crepe Cups

Crepes:
3 eggs
⅔ cup flour
½ teaspoon salt
1 cup milk

Filling:
1½ cups shredded sharp cheddar cheese
3 tablespoons flour
3 eggs, slightly beaten
⅔ cup mayonnaise
10 ounces frozen chopped spinach, thawed and drained
4-ounce can mushrooms, drained
6 bacon slices, cooked crisp and crumbled
½ teaspoon salt
Dash pepper

For crepes: combine eggs, flour, salt and milk in blender. Let stand for 1 hour in refrigerator. For 12 crepes, pour 2 tablespoons batter onto hot lightly greased 8-inch skillet. Cook on one side only, until underside is lightly browned.

For filling: toss cheese with flour, add remaining ingredients; mix well.

Fit crepes into greased muffin pan; fill with cheese mixture. Bake at 350° for 40 minutes. Serves 6.

Yellow Squash Souffle

¼ cup butter or margarine
¼ cup all-purpose flour
1⅓ cups milk
½ teaspoon salt
Dash of red pepper
1 tablespoon minced onion
1¼ cups grated yellow squash
5 eggs, separated
1 teaspoon cream of tartar
½ cup shredded sharp cheddar cheese

Melt butter in a heavy saucepan over low heat; add flour, stirring until smooth. Cook 1 minute, stirring constantly. Gradually add milk; cook over medium heat, stirring constantly, until thickened and bubbly. Stir in salt, pepper and onion; remove from heat, and let cool.

Squeeze grated squash in paper towels to remove as much liquid as possible; stir squash into sauce. Beat egg yolks until thick and lemon colored; add to squash mixture and stir well.

Beat room temperature egg whites and cream of tartar until stiff but not dry; fold into squash mixture. Pour into a 2-quart souffle dish. Bake at 350° for 1 hour; sprinkle with cheddar cheese and bake an additional 5 minutes or until a knife inserted in center comes out clean. Serves 6 to 8.

Stir-Fried Vegetables

2 teaspoons cornstarch
½ teaspoon chicken-flavored bouillon granules
½ cup water
2 tablespoons dry sherry
1 tablespoon reduced-sodium soy sauce
1 teaspoon sesame oil
1 clove garlic, minced
1 cup sweet red pepper strips
¼ teaspoon peeled, grated gingerroot
1 cup bean sprouts
2½ cups sliced squash
1 cup sliced green onions
6 ounces frozen snow pea pods, thawed

Combine first 5 ingredients; set aside. Heat oil in wok on medium high for 1 minute. Add garlic, red pepper and ginger; stir-fry 3 minutes or until crisp-tender. Add bean sprouts, squash, onions and pea pods; stir-fry 2 minutes. Pour cornstarch mixture over vegetables; stir-fry until thickened. Serve immediately. Serves 8.

Spicy Vegetable Enchiladas

8 6-inch flour tortillas
2 medium carrots, thinly sliced
1½ teaspoons chili powder
1 tablespoon cooking oil
2 cups diced zucchini
3½ ounces dark red kidney beans, drained
15 ounces salsa, divided
6 ounces Monterey Jack cheese with jalapeno peppers, shredded, divided
Cooking spray

Wrap tortillas in foil; heat in a 350° oven 10 minutes or until warm. Set aside.

Stir-fry carrots and chili powder in hot oil for 2 minutes. Add zucchini and stir-fry for 2 to 3 minutes or until crisp-tender, adding more oil if necessary. Remove from heat; stir in kidney beans, half of the salsa and half of the cheese. Spoon vegetable mixture onto tortillas, dividing it evenly. Roll up tortillas; place tortillas, seam side down, in a 2-quart rectangular baking dish which has been coated with cooking spray; cover with foil. Bake at 350° for 7 to 12 minutes or until heated through and tortillas are crisp.

Heat remaining salsa in small saucepan. Spoon over enchiladas, top with remaining cheese. Return to oven and bake just long enough for cheese to melt. Serves 4.

Broccoli Casserole
for a Crowd

2 large onions
1 stick butter
6 packages frozen chopped broccoli
4 cups cream of mushroom soup
3 packages garlic cheese
1 large can mushrooms
1 cup chopped almonds
1 cup bread crumbs

Saute onions in butter, add broccoli and cook until tender. Add soup, cheese, mushrooms and almonds. Top with bread crumbs and additional almonds, if desired. Bake in a 4-quart casserole at 325° until bubbly. Serves 18.

When cooking green beans, add a whole onion for flavor but be sure to discard it before serving.

Wonderful Sweet Potatoes

6 sweet potatoes, cooked and mashed
1¼ cups sugar
1 stick margarine
1 teaspoon salt
1 tablespoon whiskey
1 stick butter
1 cup sugar
½ cup cream
1 teaspoon vanilla
Nuts

Mix first 5 ingredients. Set aside. Melt butter, add sugar and cook until light brown. Add cream and vanilla; boil 2 minutes. Pour over mashed potatoes and heat thoroughly. Add nuts, if desired.

Donna's Potato Casserole

6 to 8 medium potatoes, cooked and diced
1 small onion, chopped
2 slices of white bread, cubed
½ green pepper, chopped
1 small jar pimiento, drained
½ pound Velveeta cheese
1 tablespoon dried parsley
½ cup butter
½ cup milk
½ cup crushed corn flakes

Mix first 7 ingredients in bowl. Place in 9 x 12 buttered casserole. Melt butter in pan, add milk to butter and pour over potato mixture. Top with crushed corn flakes. Bake at 375° for 30 minutes.

Creamed Cabbage

1 medium head cabbage
½ cup boiling water, salted
3 tablespoons butter
3 tablespoons flour
1½ cups milk
½ cup bread crumbs

Shred cabbage and cook 10 minutes in salted water. Drain, place in casserole. Melt butter over low heat, stir in flour until smooth, gradually adding milk. Cook and stir until thickened. Pour over cabbage. Top with bread crumbs. Bake at 325° for 15 minutes.

Spicy Hot Black-eyed Peas

½ cup chopped onion
½ cup chopped green pepper
15.8 ounces black-eyed peas, undrained
14.5 ounces no-salt-added stewed tomatoes, undrained
1 teaspoon dry mustard
½ teaspoon chili powder
⅛ teaspoon red pepper
½ teaspoon pepper
1 tablespoon low-sodium soy sauce
1 teaspoon liquid smoke
1 tablespoon minced fresh parsley

Coat a large, nonstick skillet with cooking spray; place over
medium heat until hot. Add onion and green pepper; saute until
vegetables are crisp-tender. Add peas and next 7 ingredients;
bring to a boil. Reduce heat and simmer 20 minutes, stirring
often. Transfer to a serving dish; sprinkle with parsley. Serves 5.

Fried Carrots

¾ cup cornmeal
¾ cup plain flour
1 teaspoon onion powder
2 tablespoons chopped parsley
Salt and pepper
1 egg white
⅔ cup buttermilk
½ teaspoon hot sauce
4 carrots, cut in thin strips

Combine cornmeal, flour, onion powder and parsley. Season
with salt and pepper. Set aside. Beat egg white until foamy. Stir
in buttermilk and hot sauce. Dip carrots in buttermilk mixture
and dredge in cornmeal mixture. Drop into 1 inch of cooking oil
at 350°; cook 2 minutes, until lightly browned.

Potato Puffs

½ cup flour
½ teaspoon salt
1 teaspoon baking powder
2 eggs, well beaten
1 cup mashed potatoes
1 tablespoon finely chopped onion

Mix and drop from teaspoon into deep hot fat and fry to a golden brown.

Entrees

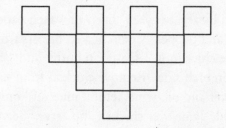

Chicken Scallopini

1 pound boneless chicken breasts
¼ cup plain flour
Salt and pepper
2 teaspoons butter
2 tablespoons cooking oil
3 tablespoons white wine
3 tablespoons fresh lemon juice
¼ cup chopped green onion

Pound chicken breasts between sheets of waxed paper. Season flour with salt and pepper. Coat chicken breasts with flour mixture. Saute chicken in 1 teaspoon butter and 1 teaspoon oil 3 to 5 minutes on each side. Remove chicken from skillet and add remaining butter and oil, wine, lemon juice and onion. Boil until slightly reduced. Pour over chicken and serve. Serves 2 to 3.

*F*or easy fried chicken without the mess—melt a stick of margarine in a 9 x 12 inch baking dish, roll chicken in Bisquick and crushed corn flakes, then turn in melted butter and bake 1 hour at 400°.

Chicken Pot Pie

Pastry for top
3 chicken breasts, cooked and chopped
1 can mixed peas and carrots
4 boiled eggs, chopped
1 stick margarine
8 tablespoons flour
1 teaspoon salt
Pepper
4 cups chicken broth

Cover bottom of casserole with chicken. Drain peas and carrots and add to chicken. Add chopped eggs. Melt margarine; stir in flour and season with salt and pepper. Add chicken broth and cook until thick. Pour over chicken, cover with thick pastry and dot with margarine. Cook at 350° for 30 minutes, then brown top crust at 400° for 5 minutes.

Jo's Chicken Divan

20 ounces frozen broccoli, cooked and drained
3 chicken breasts, cooked and boned
2 cans cream of chicken soup
1 cup mayonnaise
½ cup shredded sharp cheese
1 can mushrooms, optional
½ cup bread crumbs
Parmesan cheese
1 can water chestnuts
1 teaspoon curry powder
½ stick melted butter
Juice of 1 lemon

Arrange broccoli in a 9 x 13 baking dish. Place chicken on top of broccoli. Combine next 8 ingredients and pour over chicken. Top with melted butter and sprinkle lemon juice over all. Bake at 350° for 1 hour and 15 minutes. Serves 6 to 8.

Edna's Chicken and Dressing

3½ cups herb stuffing mix
3 cups cooked chicken
½ cup margarine
½ cup flour
¼ teaspoon salt
4 cups chicken broth
6 eggs, beaten
Pimiento Mushroom Sauce

Prepare stuffing mix according to directions and spread in 9 x 12 casserole. Add chicken. Melt margarine in a large saucepan. Blend in flour, salt and broth. Cook until mixture thickens. Stir small amount of hot mixture into eggs, return to hot mixture and remove from heat. Pour over chicken in casserole. Bake at 325° for 40 to 45 minutes. Cut into squares and serve with sauce.

Pimiento Mushroom Sauce:
1 can mushroom soup
¼ cup milk
1 cup sour cream
¼ cup chopped pimiento

Combine all ingredients; heat and serve with above.

Chicken Crepes

Crepes:
2 eggs
1 cup milk
⅓ cup margarine, melted
1 cup flour

Filling:
3 cups cooked chicken, diced
¾ cup Half & Half
1 tablespoon parsley
1 tablespoon minced onion
2 egg yolks, beaten
2 tablespoons shredded Swiss cheese
2 tablespoons Parmesan cheese

For crepes: mix all ingredients in blender, refrigerate 1 hour before cooking. Pour ⅓ cup batter in a lightly greased 8-inch skillet. Batter will be similar to pancakes, only lighter.

For filling: mix first five ingredients. Place 3 tablespoons of this mixture in crepe; roll and place in buttered baking dish. Pour 1 ½ cups Veloute Sauce* over crepes, sprinkle with cheese.

*Veloute Sauce:
6 tablespoons butter
6 tablespoons flour
3 cups strained chicken broth
¾ teaspoon salt

Cook until thick.

Governor's Mansion Chicken Salad

4 cups diced cooked chicken, cold
2 tablespoons lemon juice
¾ cup mayonnaise
1 teaspoon salt
2 cups chopped celery
4 hard-boiled eggs, sliced
¾ cup cream of chicken soup
1 teaspoon finely chopped onion
2 pimentos, cut fine (1 small jar)
1 cup grated cheese
1½ cups crushed potato chips
⅔ cup finely chopped almonds

Combine all ingredients except cheese, potato chips and almonds.
Place in a large baking dish, top with cheese, chips and almonds.
Let stand overnight in refrigerator. Bake at 400° for 20 to 25
minutes. Serves 8.

Chicken and Wild Rice Casserole

3 cups cubed cooked chicken breast
1 package Uncle Ben's Long Grain and Wild Rice
¼ cup butter
⅓ cup chopped onion
⅓ cup flour
Salt and pepper
1 cup Half & Half
1 cup chicken broth
⅓ cup chopped pimiento
⅓ cup chopped parsley
¼ cup chopped almonds
⅓ cup mushrooms

Prepare cooked chicken, measure and set aside. Prepare rice according to package directions and set aside. Melt butter in large saucepan. Saute onions; stir in flour, salt and pepper. Gradually add Half & Half and chicken broth. Cook, stirring constantly, until thickened. Stir in chicken, pimientos, parsley, almonds, mushrooms and cooked rice. Place in a 2-quart casserole. Bake at 425° for 30 minutes. Serves 6 to 8.

Hot or Cold Paella Salad

5 ounces saffron rice mix
2 tablespoons wine vinegar
⅓ cup salad oil
1 teaspoon dry mustard
Salt, to taste
2½ cups chopped cooked chicken
1 cup chopped tomatoes
¾ cup chopped green peppers
1 cup cooked green peas
⅛ cup onion
⅓ cup chopped celery
4-ounce jar drained pimiento
⅓ cup sliced pitted olives
⅛ teaspoon Tabasco sauce
½ pound cooked shrimp, optional
½ pound cooked ham, optional

Cook rice according to package directions. Combine vinegar, oil and dry mustard. Season to taste with salt; pour over rice and refrigerate. Mix remaining ingredients and refrigerate. Add to rice when all is cold.

Dressing:
1 cup mayonnaise
1 teaspoon turmeric
½ teaspoon salt
2 tablespoons lemon juice

Blend all ingredients in blender and serve in separate dish.

Note: this may be served cold on lettuce or heated as a casserole.

Michael's Ginger Chicken

4 boneless chicken breasts, skinned
12 ounces pineapple juice
1 teaspoon garlic powder
⅓ cup soy sauce
½ teaspoon confectioners' sugar

Place chicken in glass container or zip-lock bag. Mix remaining ingredients, pour over chicken and marinate in refrigerator overnight. Baste with marinade while grilling, or bake at 400° for 15 to 20 minutes. Serves 4.

Rotel Chicken

3 cups cooked chicken
Reserved chicken broth
23 ounces vermicelli spaghetti
1 can rotel tomatoes
1 pound Velveeta cheese, cut into 1" chunks
1 can mushrooms
2 large bell peppers, chopped
2 large onions, chopped
1 stick margarine

Prepare and measure chicken, retaining broth to cook spaghetti.
Set chicken aside. Cook spaghetti in chicken broth. Saute
mushrooms, peppers and onions in margarine. Mix chicken,
spaghetti and remaining ingredients together in large casserole
dish. Bake at 350° until hot. Serves 6 to 8.

Tennessee Chicken Pot Pie

1 regular size can Veg All vegetables, drained
2 cans cream of potato soup
¼ cup milk
Salt and pepper to taste
2 cups diced, cooked chicken
1 partially cooked pie shell
1 uncooked pie shell

Mix all ingredients and pour into pie shell, then top with second pie shell (uncooked) and bake at 350° for 25 minutes. Serves 4.

Chicken and Noodle Casserole

5 to 6 chicken breasts, boiled
4 to 5 green onions
2 tablespoons butter
12 ounces fettucine, egg or spinach or half of each
Chicken broth, reserved from cooking chicken
2 tablespoons butter
Fresh grated Parmesan

Sauce:
1 cup Hellman's mayonnaise
1 cup sour cream
1 can cream of mushroom soup
1½ teaspoons Dijon mustard
3 tablespoons dry sherry
6 ounces medium sharp cheddar cheese, grated

Remove bones from cooked chicken and set aside. Saute green onions in butter and mix with chicken. Cook fettucine as directed on package, using chicken broth instead of water. Drain and toss with butter.

Combine all sauce ingredients and mix well. Place noodles in large casserole dish. Cover with chicken/onion mixture. Top with sauce mixture. Sprinkle generously with fresh Parmesan. Bake at 350° for 35 minutes (top will be light brown). Serves 6.

Praline Ham

1 cooked ham, 6 to 8 pounds
1½ cups maple syrup
½ cup sugar
2 tablespoons butter or margarine
1 cup chopped pecans

Score outside of ham in a diamond pattern. Place ham in shallow baking pan, fat side up. Insert meat thermometer, making sure it does not touch fat or bone. Bake, uncovered, at 325° for 2 hours or until thermometer registers 140°.

Combine syrup, sugar, and butter in a small saucepan; bring to a boil. Stir in pecans. Remove from heat. Spoon sauce over ham and bake an additional 15 minutes. Serve remaining sauce with ham. Serves 12.

Instead of frying country ham, place two or three slices in heavy aluminum foil and bake about an hour. It's tender and does not make a mess.

Marinated Beef Tenderloin

1 cup catsup
2 teaspoons prepared mustard
½ teaspoon Worcestershire sauce
1½ cups water
1.4 ounces Italian salad dressing mix
4- to 6-pound beef tenderloin, trimmed
Watercress, optional
Red and white grapes, optional

Combine first 5 ingredients; mix well. Spear meat in several places and place in a zip-lock plastic bag. Pour marinade over meat and seal bag. Place in a shallow pan and refrigerate 8 hours, turning occasionally.

Drain and reserve marinade. Place tenderloin on a rack in baking pan. Bake at 425° for 30 to 45 minutes, basting occasionally with marinade while baking. Remove to serving platter and garnish with watercress and grapes. Serve remaining marinade with meat. Serves 12 to 15.

Meat Loaf

3 slices bread
1 cup milk
2 eggs
1 small onion, finely chopped
Salt and pepper
10 ounces cream of celery soup
1½ pounds ground beef
3 tablespoons brown sugar
¼ cup catsup
1 teaspoon dry mustard

Break bread into small pieces and soak in milk. Add eggs, onion, salt, pepper and soup. Mix well and add ground beef. Mix thoroughly and mold in loaf pan. Combine brown sugar, catsup and mustard. Spread mixture over meat loaf. Bake at 350° for 1 hour. Serves 8.

Lasagna

1 pound lean ground chuck
1 cup chopped onion
3 cloves garlic, finely chopped
4 cups tomato juice
8 ounces mushrooms, optional
1 can tomato paste
1 teaspoon oregano leaves
1 teaspoon parsley flakes
½ teaspoon salt
⅛ teaspoon pepper
8 ounces lasagna noodles, uncooked
16 ounces small curd cottage cheese
1½ cups grated Parmesan cheese
2 cups shredded Mozzarella cheese
Parsley flakes

Preheat oven to 350°. Brown meat in large saucepan; add onion
and garlic; drain off fat. Stir in tomato juice, mushrooms, tomato
paste and seasonings. Simmer 30 minutes, stirring occasionally.
In a 9 x 13 baking dish, layer ½ each of the uncooked noodles,
sauce and three cheeses. Repeat layering; top with parsley. Cover
with aluminum foil and bake 30 minutes. Remove foil; continue
baking, uncovered, an additional 15 minutes. Remove from oven
and let stand 20 minutes before cutting. Serves 6 to 8.

Note: lasagna can be prepared ahead and refrigerated. Bake,
covered, 45 minutes; uncover and continue baking 15 minutes.

 Shish Kebabs

1½ pounds beef round, cut in 1" cubes
1 teaspoon ground ginger, optional
2 cloves garlic, crushed
2 tablespoons brown sugar
½ cup soy sauce
2 tablespoons vegetable oil
Ground black pepper, to taste

Place meat in glass bowl or zip-lock bag. Combine all sauce
ingredients. Pour over meat, coating well and marinate in
refrigerator for 24 to 48 hours, turning occasionally. Place meat
on skewers; grill, basting often.

*T*o stretch that
potato salad, add
chopped lettuce—
good and it feeds
more folks!

Church Supper Casserole

1½ pounds ground beef
½ cup chopped onion
12 ounces whole kernel corn, drained
11 ounces cheddar cheese soup, undiluted
1 cup sour cream
¼ cup chopped pimiento
½ teaspoon salt
½ teaspoon pepper
3 cups cooked, drained noodles
Cracker crumbs
½ cup shredded cheddar cheese
3 tablespoons butter

Brown ground beef in skillet, add onion and cook until tender. Stir in corn, soup, sour cream, pimiento, salt, pepper and noodles. Place in a 2 quart casserole, cover with cracker crumbs and cheese. Dot with butter. Bake at 350° for 30 minutes. Serves 6 to 8.

Stuffed Cabbage

1 large head cabbage
1½ pounds ground chuck
2 onions, chopped
2 to 3 cloves garlic, chopped
Vegetable oil
1 cup rice
2 cups water
½ teaspoon salt
½ teaspoon pepper
2 eggs, beaten
3 tablespoons tomato sauce
1 can sauerkraut
3 or 4 strips bacon, uncooked
16 ounces tomato sauce

Remove as much core from cabbage as possible. Steam leaves in boiling water over low heat. Brown ground chuck. Saute onions and garlic in vegetable oil; add to ground chuck. Cook rice in water until partially done. Drain and mix into ground meat; add salt, pepper, eggs and tomato sauce. Mix well. Place mixture by tablespoonfuls into cabbage leaves, roll and fold over ends.

Place ½ can sauerkraut on bottom of a large Dutch oven or stockpot. Layer stuffed cabbage rolls over sauerkraut. Place remaining sauerkraut over top along with remainder of chopped sweet cabbage. Place bacon over top of cabbage. Cover with tomato sauce and add enough water to cover all. Cover and simmer over low heat about 2 hours.

Great with mashed potatoes!

Sour Cream Noodle Bake

4 cups medium egg noodles
1 pound ground beef
8 ounces tomato sauce
1 teaspoon salt
¼ teaspoon garlic salt
⅛ teaspoon pepper
2 cups sour cream
1 cup thinly sliced green onions
1 cup shredded cheddar cheese

Cook noodles as directed on package. Set aside. Brown ground beef and drain. Add tomato sauce, salt, pepper and garlic salt to beef. Simmer, uncovered, for 5 minutes.

In a separate dish, mix noodles, sour cream and onions. Shred extra cheddar cheese and mix in as well. Butter a 2-quart casserole dish. Layer noodles and beef alternately, starting with noodles and ending with beef. Sprinkle cheddar cheese on top. Bake at 350° for 25 minutes. Serves 6.

Easy Pork Chop Dinner

4 to 6 pork chops
Cooking oil
1 to 1½ cups uncooked rice
Sliced tomato
Sliced green peppers
Sliced onions
1 to 1½ cups beef bouillon

In skillet, brown pork chops in a small amount of oil. Remove from skillet, cover bottom with rice; layer pork chops over rice. Place one slice of tomato, green pepper and onion on each pork chop. Cover with bouillon and cook, covered, on low heat until rice is done and pork chops are tender, about 45 minutes. Serves 4 to 6.

Meatball Skillet Dinner

2 strips bacon
1 pound ground beef
1 teaspoon salt
¼ teaspoon pepper
1 onion
1 green pepper
1 can kidney beans
10 ounces tomato soup
½ soup can of water
1 tablespoon chili powder
2 cups cooked elbow macaroni

Cook bacon, ground beef, salt and pepper in skillet until beef is browned. Cut onion and green pepper into strips and add to meat in skillet. Add remaining ingredients. Cook for 15 minutes and serve.

*T*ry adding a package of onion soup mix to hamburgers for grilling. The taste is great.

Oriental Pepper Steak

1½ pounds beef, cut in strips
1 teaspoon salt
¼ cup oil
1 cup beef bouillon
½ teaspoon sugar
¼ teaspoon ginger
1 teaspoon soy sauce
2 green peppers, cut into thin strips
1 medium onion, cut into thin strips
2 teaspoons cornstarch
2 tablespoons water

Sprinkle beef with salt and brown in hot oil. Set aside. In saucepan, combine bouillon, sugar, ginger and soy sauce. Bring to boil, simmer 15 minutes. Add vegetables to skillet, sprinkle with salt. Mix cornstarch and water to make paste. Gradually add bouillon mixture and cornstarch to beef mixture, stirring constantly until mixture thickens. Serve with noodles or cooked rice.

Veal Scallopini

1⅓ pounds veal, thinly sliced
Flour
Salt
Pepper
½ cup butter
¼ cup Marsala wine
3 tablespoons canned concentrated bouillon

Pound veal until thin. Dip in flour seasoned with salt and pepper. Heat butter in heavy skillet, add veal and brown. Add wine and cook 1 minute longer. Transfer meat to warm serving dish. Add bouillon to pan drippings, bring to boil and pour over meat. Serves 4.

Snapper with Dill Sauce

4 snapper fillets, 4 ounces each
2 tablespoons olive oil
Salt
Pepper

Brush snapper with 1 tablespoon oil, sprinkle with salt and pepper. Let stand 15 minutes. Pan fry fish in 1 tablespoon oil, 3 to 5 minutes. Serve fillets over cooked rice, covered with dill sauce. Serves 4.

Creamy Dill Sauce:
10 ounces refrigerated Alfredo sauce
2 tablespoons Chablis or dry white wine
1 teaspoon dried dillweed

Combine all ingredients in heavy saucepan, cook until thoroughly heated.

Shrimp Spaghetti

8 ounces spaghetti
1 stick butter
Garlic salt
4 ounces freshly sliced mushrooms
½ to 1 pound shrimp, peeled
4 tablespoons grated Romano cheese
Salt and pepper, to taste

Cook spaghetti, drain and set aside. Melt butter in large skillet, add garlic salt and mushrooms. Saute mushrooms; add shrimp and cook slowly for 5 minutes. Add spaghetti to skillet; cover with Romano cheese and season with salt and pepper. Fold spaghetti over from edge of skillet to center until heated throughout. Serves 4.

Linguine and Shrimp

½ pound linguine
½ cup Italian salad dressing
½ pound small shrimp, peeled
1 yellow squash, cut into strips
1 zucchini, cut into strips
Carrots, cut into strips
3 green onions
2 teaspoons lemon juice
Dash cayenne pepper

Cook linguine as directed on package. Heat dressing in skillet, add remaining ingredients except linguine; cook 10 minutes. Add linguine and toss. Serves 4.

Sweet-and-Sour Shrimp

1½ pounds fresh, medium shrimp
1 tablespoon vegetable oil
¼ cup chopped sweet red pepper
¼ cup sliced green onions
1 clove garlic, minced
⅓ cup red plum jam
2 tablespoons dry white wine
2 tablespoons white vinegar
2 tablespoons cocktail sauce
2 tablespoons chutney
½ teaspoon salt
¼ teaspoon crushed red pepper
¼ pound fresh snow pea pods
Hot cooked rice

Peel and devein shrimp; set aside. Combine oil, pepper, onions and garlic in a 1½ quart baking dish. Microwave, uncovered, on high for 2 to 3 minutes or until tender, stirring at 1-minute intervals. Add shrimp. Cover with plastic wrap, leaving a small hole at the edge of bowl for steam to escape. Microwave on medium for 8 to 10 minutes or until shrimp are opaque and firm, stirring at 3-minute intervals. Drain.

Combine next 7 ingredients; stir well. Pour over shrimp and stir gently. Cover and microwave on high for 1 to 1½ minutes to heat sauce. Add snow peas; mix gently. Cover and microwave on high for 2 to 2½ minutes or until snow peas are crisp-tender. Serve over cooked rice. Serves 4.

Crab Cakes

3 ounces country ham
¼ cup egg substitute
1 tablespoon baking powder
1 teaspoon Old Bay seasoning
1 tablespoon chopped fresh parsley
1 tablespoon reduced sodium Worcestershire sauce
1 tablespoon reduced fat mayonnaise
2 slices white bread
1 pound fresh jumbo lump crabmeat, drained
Vegetable cooking spray
Lemon slices

Trim ham and slice thin. Place in a large nonstick skillet; add water to cover. Cook over high heat for 3 minutes. Remove ham from skillet and drain. Chop ham finely and set aside.

Combine egg substitute and next 5 ingredients in a large bowl. Set aside.

Remove crusts from bread and discard. Tear bread into ½-inch pieces; add bread and ham to egg substitute mixture. Let stand until liquid is absorbed. Stir well. Fold in crabmeat and shape into 8 patties. Cook in a nonstick skillet coated with cooking spray until lightly browned, turning once. Serves 8.

Crabmeat Crepes

Crepes:
2 eggs
1 cup milk
⅓ cup melted margarine
1 cup flour

Filling:
¼ cup chopped onion
¼ cup butter
¼ cup flour
1 tablespoon prepared mustard
1 tablespoon chopped parsley
1 tablespoon Worcestershire sauce
1 tablespoon chili sauce
½ cup milk
1 egg, beaten
½ pound cooked crabmeat

For crepes: mix all ingredients in blender; refrigerate 1 hour. Lightly grease an 8-inch skillet, place ¼ or ⅓ cup batter in hot skillet. Cook until set, turning once as you would a pancake.

For filling: saute onions in butter; add flour, mustard, parsley, Worcestershire sauce and chili sauce. Add milk and cook over low heat until thick. Stir a small amount of thickened mixture into beaten egg. Pour egg mixture into heated mixture. Cook, stirring constantly. Add crabmeat. Fill crepes with mixture, fold over, brush with 2 tablespoons melted butter. Heat at 350° for 10 to 15 minutes. Makes 16 crepes.

Fettucine Alfredo

1 pound noodles
¼ pound real butter
4 handfuls Parmesan cheese
½ pint whipping cream, whipped

Cook noodles according to package directions. Melt butter, add cheese and whipped cream. Place 1 large scoop on hot serving dish. Add noodles and remaining mixture.

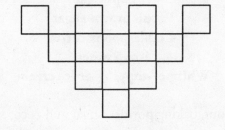

Baked Chocolate Pudding

1 cup flour
2 tablespoons baking powder
¾ cup sugar
1½ tablespoons cocoa
½ cup milk
1 teaspoon vanilla
2 tablespoons melted margarine
½ cup nuts
½ cup sugar
½ cup brown sugar
4 tablespoons cocoa
1 cup water
Whipped topping or ice cream

Sift together flour, baking powder, sugar and cocoa. Add milk, vanilla, melted margarine and nuts. Pour into a 9 x 9 baking dish. Mix together sugar, brown sugar and cocoa. Sprinkle over top of batter in dish. Top with water. Bake at 350° for 1 hour. Serve with whipped topping or ice cream.

Easy Dessert

1 large can sliced peaches
1 box Betty Crocker Butter Brickle cake mix
1 stick margarine, melted
1 teaspoon vanilla
Nuts, optional

Pour peaches with juice into 9 x 13 pan. Sprinkle cake mix over peaches. Combine margarine and vanilla, drizzle over top of cake mix. Sprinkle nuts on top, if desired. Bake at 350° for 45 minutes. Serve with whipped topping.

Blueberry or Cherry Dessert

1⅓ cups coarsely crushed pretzels
1 stick + 2 tablespoons melted margarine
⅓ cup sugar
8 ounces cream cheese
1 carton whipped topping
¼ cup confectioners' sugar
1 can pie filling

Place crushed pretzels in bottom of 8 or 9-inch square pan.
Mix melted margarine and sugar. Drizzle mixture over crushed
pretzels. Bake at 325° for 10 minutes. Mix cream cheese,
whipped topping and confectioners' sugar. Pour over pretzels.
Chill and serve topped with pie filling of your choice.

Angel Delight

½ Angel food cake
3¾ ounces vanilla pudding mix
3 cups milk
1 teaspoon vanilla
8 ounces pineapple chunks
1 can coconut
1 jar maraschino cherries
1 cup pecans

Break angel food cake into small pieces. Combine pudding mix, milk, and vanilla; shake or mix according to package directions. In a glass container, layer cake, pudding, pineapple, coconut, cherries and pecans. Refrigerate overnight.

Easy Pie Crust

1 cup self rising flour
⅓ cup cooking oil
3 tablespoons milk

Place all ingredients directly into pie pan and mix. Press dough to shape around pie pan. If your recipe calls for a baked crust, bake at 350° for 3 to 4 minutes to set, then fill. Very flaky.

*I*nstead of dropping chocolate chip cookie dough by spoonfuls, try spreading the entire bowl of dough onto a greased cookie sheet; you'll finish baking more quickly.

Strawberry Pie

1 cup sugar
3 tablespoons flour or cornstarch
4 tablespoons strawberry Jello
1 cup boiling water
Strawberries, washed and capped
Baked pie crust
Whipped topping

Combine sugar and flour or cornstarch and Jello. Pour boiling
water over and cook until thick. Place washed strawberries in
prepared pie crust. Pour glaze mixture over strawberries.
Refrigerate for 2 hours. Serve with whipped topping.

Chess Pie

1 stick margarine
1½ cups sugar
1½ teaspoons cornmeal
1½ teaspoons vinegar
3 eggs, slightly beaten
1 teaspoon vanilla
Unbaked pie shell

Mix margarine, sugar, cornmeal and vinegar in pan over low heat, let cool slightly. Add eggs and vanilla. Pour into pie shell and bake at 325° for 45 minutes.

Martha Lewis' Peach Pie

1 egg
⅓ cup melted margerine
⅓ cup flour
1 cup sugar
1 teaspoon vanilla
3 to 4 fresh peaches, sliced
Unbaked pie crust

Mix first five ingredients. Place sliced peaches in crust. Pour mixture over peaches. Bake at 350° for 1 hour.

Pineapple Pie

2 cups sugar
4 tablespoons flour
2 eggs, well beaten
1 stick margarine
1 small can crushed pineapple
1 unbaked pie shell

Stir all ingredients together and pour into pie shell. Bake at 425° for 15 minutes; reduce oven temperature to 325° and bake for an additional 30 minutes.

Pecan Pie

3 eggs, slightly beaten
1 cup white syrup
1 cup sugar
2 tablespoons melted margarine
1 teaspoon vanilla
1½ cups pecans
1 unbaked pie shell

Mix first 5 ingredients, add pecans. Pour into pie shell and bake at 350° for 50 to 55 minutes.

Fudge Pie

¼ cup melted margarine
¼ cup flour
1 cup sugar
3 tablespoons cocoa
2 eggs
1 teaspoon vanilla

Mix all ingredients, add chopped nuts if desired. Pour into a lightly greased and floured pie pan. Bake at 300° for 30 minutes.

*I*t's a good idea to keep vanilla ice cream and a dry package of whipped topping on hand to dress up desserts such as pies, cakes, Irish coffee— plus preserves for sundaes.

Peanut Butter Pie

8 ounces cream cheese
14 ounces sweetened condensed milk
2 teaspoons vanilla
¾ cup peanut butter
8 ounces non-dairy whipped topping
10-inch graham cracker crust

Combine cream cheese, milk, vanilla and peanut butter. Mix with electric mixer until smooth. Fold in whipped topping and pour into shell. Decorate with chocolate syrup or sprinkle with mini-chocolate chips if desired. Refrigerate or freeze. Serves 8.

Variation: For a low-fat dessert, use low-fat or no-fat ingredients. Same great taste, less fattening.

Apple Pie

1 can apple pie filling
1½ cups sugar
½ cup orange juice
1 stick margarine
Unbaked pastry shell
Pastry strips for top

Boil sugar, margarine and orange juice. Cut apple into smaller pieces and place in unbaked pastry shell. Pour heated mixture over apples. Top with pastry strips and bake at 325° for 40 to 45 minutes.

This makes 1 big pie or 2 small ones. For a slight variation, add 2 teaspoons crushed pineapple.

Apple Cake

2 eggs
1 cup white sugar
1 cup brown sugar
1¼ cups salad oil
3 cups plain flour
1 teaspoon soda
1 teaspoon cinnamon
2 teaspoons vanilla
1 cup chopped pecans
3 cups chopped apples

Mix first 8 ingredients in the order listed. Add pecans and apples. Bake in a greased and floured tube pan at 350° for 1 hour and 15 minutes.

Hummingbird Cake

3 cups plain flour
2 cups sugar
1 teaspoon baking soda
1 teaspoon salt
1 teaspoon ground cinnamon
3 eggs, beaten
1 cup vegetable oil
1½ teaspoons vanilla
8 ounces crushed pineapple, undrained
2 cups chopped bananas
1 cup chopped pecans

Frosting:
8 ounces cream cheese
½ cup butter
16 ounces confectioners' sugar
1 teaspoon vanilla
½ cup chopped pecans

Combine first 5 ingredients in a large bowl. Add eggs, oil and vanilla; mix well, but do not beat. Stir in pineapple, nuts and bananas. Spoon into 3 greased and floured 9-inch round pans. Bake at 350° for 25 to 30 minutes. Cool completely.

For frosting: beat cream cheese and butter until smooth. Add sugar and vanilla, and mix well. Add nuts to frosting or sprinkle on top of cake after frosting the cake.

Coconut Cake

1 package yellow or white cake mix
2 cups sugar
16 ounces sour cream
12 ounces frozen coconut, thawed
1 small container non-dairy topping, thawed

Prepare and bake cake mix according to package directions. Allow to cool. Split baked cake to make 4 layers. Combine remaining ingredients, spread over each layer and top of cake. Refrigerate about 3 days before serving.

Chocolate Pound Cake

1 cup butter or margarine, softened
1 cup shortening
3 cups sugar
5 large eggs
3 cups all-purpose flour
¼ cup cocoa
½ teaspoon baking powder
½ teaspoon salt
1 cup milk
1 tablespoon vanilla extract

Beat butter and shortening with an electric mixer until creamy.
Gradually add sugar, beating at medium speed 5 to 7 minutes.
Add eggs, one at a time, beating just until yellow disappears.
Combine flour and next 3 ingredients; add to butter mixture
alternately with milk, beginning and ending with flour mixture.
Mix at low speed just until blended after each addition. Stir in
vanilla. Pour batter into a greased and floured 10-inch tube pan.
Bake at 325° for 1 hour and 30 minutes or until a wooden
toothpick inserted in center of cake comes out clean. Cool in pan
10 to 15 minutes; remove and completely cool on wire rack.

Blackberry Walnut Cake

2 cups sugar
1 cup butter
4 eggs
3 cups plain flour
2 teaspoons baking powder
1 teaspoon salt
1 teaspoon cinnamon
1 cup milk
1 cup blackberry jam
½ to ¾ cup nuts

Icing:
½ stick margarine
1 box confectioners' sugar
1 egg white, unbeaten
2 to 3 tablespoons sherry

Cream butter, sugar and eggs. Add flour and spices. Alternate dry ingredients with milk into creamed mixture. Add jam and nuts. Bake in a greased and floured stem pan at 350° for 1 hour 15 minutes. Frost when completely cooled.

For icing: combine margarine, sugar and egg white. Add sherry and remaining sugar.

Sock It To Me Cake

1 box yellow cake mix
8 ounces sour cream
4 eggs
½ cup sugar
⅔ cup cooking oil
1 tablespoon vanilla
1 cup nuts
2 tablespoons cinnamon
2 tablespoons brown sugar

Mix first seven ingredients. Pour ½ of batter into a greased and
floured bundt pan. Combine cinnamon and brown sugar.
Sprinkle ½ of this mixture over batter in pan. Cover with
remaining batter. Top with remaining cinnamon/sugar mixture.
Bake at 350° for 1 hour.

Butterfinger Cookies

1 stick margarine
¾ cup sugar
1 egg
½ teaspoon vanilla
1 ¼ cups flour
½ teaspoon salt
½ teaspoon soda
1 cup Butterfinger candy bars, cut into small pieces

Cream margarine and sugar, add egg and vanilla. Sift flour, salt and soda together. Mix wet and dry ingredients together and add candy pieces. Chill dough for 30 minutes. Drop by teaspoonfuls onto greased baking sheet. Bake at 350° for 10 to 12 minutes. Remove from baking sheet and cool on wire racks.

Orange Cookies

1 pound vanilla wafers, finely crushed
1 box powdered sugar, sifted
1 cup chopped pecans
1 stick margarine, melted
6 ounces frozen orange juice
Coconut, optional
Powdered sugar, optional

Mix vanilla wafers, powdered sugar and pecans together. Add margarine and orange juice and roll into small balls. Roll in coconut or additional powdered sugar and refrigerate until ready to use. Cookies may be frozen.

Chocolate Brickle Squares

Vegetable cooking spray
12 (4¾ x 2½) graham crackers
1 cup butter or margarine
1 cup sugar
12 ounces semi-sweet chocolate morsels
6 ounces almond brickle chips

Line a 15 x 10 x 1 inch pan with aluminum foil, coat with spray. Place graham crackers in a single layer in prepared pan. Set aside.

Combine butter and sugar in saucepan. Bring to boil over medium heat, stirring constantly. Boil for 1 ½ to 2 minutes, without stirring. Pour mixture over graham crackers. Bake at 350° for 5 minutes. Remove from oven and sprinkle with chocolate chips. Let stand until morsels are soft enough to spread. Spread smoothly over top. Sprinkle with brickle, press lightly. Cool and cut into 1 ½-inch squares. Yields 5 dozen.

Microwave Pralines

1 cup packed light brown sugar
1 cup granulated sugar
⅓ cup light corn syrup
¼ cup water
1 tablespoon butter or margarine
1 teaspoon vanilla extract
1½ cups pecan halves or pieces

Line a cookie sheet with foil; lightly grease foil or coat with vegetable spray. Oil a large tablespoon. Mix sugars, corn syrup and water in a 2-quart glass measure. Microwave uncovered on high 6 to 8 minutes, without stirring, until a candy thermometer reads 234° to 240°F (soft-ball stage) or a small amount dropped into very cold water forms a soft ball that flattens when removed from the water. Stir in butter and vanilla extract, then the nuts until blended. Let stand 2 minutes. Stir vigorously about 2 minutes until mixture thickens and turns from clear to opaque. Drop tablespoonfuls onto lined cookie sheet. (If mixture sets before all the pralines are made, microwave on high 45 seconds or until mixture can be stirred.) Let stand about 1 hour or until completely cooled. Remove from foil and store in an airtight container with waxed paper between layers. Makes 20.

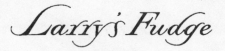

Larry's Fudge

⅔ cup cocoa
3 cups sugar
⅛ teaspoon salt
1½ cups milk
½ stick butter
1 teaspoon vanilla

Mix first four ingredients. Cook over medium heat to hard ball stage, remove from heat. Add butter and vanilla. Using a wooden spoon, beat, beat, beat. Place in lightly buttered 9 x 13 baking dish.

Divinity

¾ cup Karo syrup
4 cups sugar
¾ cup boiling water
3 egg whites
Vanilla

Cook syrup, sugar and water to 245° (firm ball stage). Beat egg whites until stiff. Gradually add boiling mixture to egg whites while still beating. Add vanilla. Drop by teaspoonfuls onto waxed paper.

Party Mints

1 box confectioners' sugar
3 tablespoons evaporated milk
½ stick margarine
5 to 12 drops peppermint oil

Mix all the above ingredients. Place in rubber or plastic molds and chill. Let set before removing.

This recipe freezes well.

*E*asy idea for shortcake for fresh fruit—prepare biscuit dough using an extra ½ cup of sugar, cut in rounds and roll them thinly, like cookies, and bake at 350° until brown.

Index to Recipes

Simply Tennessee

Mail to:
McClanahan Publishing House, Inc.
P. O. Box 100
Kuttawa, KY 42055

For Orders call TOLL FREE
1-800-544-6959
Visa & MasterCard accepted

Please send me _____ copies of

Simply Tennessee @ $ 12.95 each_____
Postage & handling   3.50

Kentucky residents add 6% sales tax @   .78 each_____

Total enclosed   _____

Make check payable to McClanahan Publishing House

Ship to:
NAME _____

ADDRESS _____

CITY _____ STATE _____ ZIP _____